Depressed & Despaired:
The Synergy of Lasting Hope?

Assumpta Onyinye Ude, PhD

CONTENTS

DEDICATION

This book is in memory of my only little Sister, Okechi Maria Gorretti Igwe whose senseless death as an infant and the events that orchestrated it triggered my inner yearning and silent search for the meaning and purpose of life. To you, the reader or anyone seeking true hope in Christ.

FOREWORD

Assumpta Onyinye Ude is an embodiment of absolute hope and confident trust in God. Her encounter with Christ in her early days of college life was so transformational that it became the springboard, from which her new life of courage and strength emerged.
I recommend this book to anyone who is seeking recovery from the damage done by ugly life experiences. If you are doing well and have no problems, the carefully crafted real-life stories contained in this book will broaden your faith and help you to relate and counsel people who have faced traumatic life experiences. Assumpta made it clear that life is not over until it is over. Only believe!

George Ude (Ph.D.) National Director, Bethel Campus Fellowship
Chair, Natural Science Department, Bowie State University

PREFACE

I wrote this book with a conviction and a personal mindset of "hoping against hope." It was the impossibilities I saw many years ago as a child in attempting to find real hope in my moments of discouragement and disappointments, which resulted in the writing of this book. The search for true hope is a universal human need.

How can you find lasting hope when overwhelmed with despair and discouragement? How? To believe there is a synergy that builds between depression and despair from hopelessness is either a superstition or a religious fantasy. If dwelling in hopelessness could breed hope, psychologists would be out of business. Moreover, we would not have to ask why God would create a world of unpredictable chaos. The God of the Bible is not a heartless recluse as may be suggestive of some people's response to pressures of life. Life is not always good but the just God that keeps covenant with humanity is good all the time. God is not the author of our painful experiences, but He allows them. He uses the ugly experiences of those that call upon Him in their days of trouble for an ironic good purpose.

When I found hope in Christ as a college student, I thought; "All is well, wonders and miracles galore all the way...no more pain, no more sorrow." Nope! I faced moments of rejection, afterward. Many people called me crazy, stupid and brainwashed! To my surprise, and unlike my old self, I was happy, undaunted and filled with joy. I was able to access *"the grace of our Lord Jesus Christ, the love of God and the fellowship of the Holy Spirit"* (2 Corinthians. 13:14).

I effortlessly forgave those who despised and insulted me because I confessed that; "I am born again"- had accepted Christ as my Savior.

I endured and overcame what naturally would have set me back to sadness and lamentation. I found hope during those tough years because I learned from the Holy Scriptures that the adversary engages people and circumstances of life to besiege the faith of believers in Christ. Like those four lepers in the gate of Samaria besieged with homelessness and stigma (2 Kings 7), Christ enabled me to take a blind step of faith into the unknown. Like the Hebrew girl Esther, I thought, *"If I perish, I perish'*, and like King David, I thought it better to fall into the Hands of the LORD than leave my destiny in human hands. God picked me up from the pit of pity partying, He lifted me and set my feet on the Solid Rock, Christ Jesus. No more *'a banished child of Eve'* as I was taught to claim, but a bold, liberated daughter of Zion. In my new life of glorious freedom, I no longer glory in my pedigree, but in my destiny with Creator God Yahweh. I am still learning from this school called 'life.' I am still running the race to eternity and have not arrived.

Many people in our homes and communities are in distress and despair. Many are wishing they could find someone to provide solution to their pains. You may think all is well with the person next to you because of the facade of happiness and smiles on Facebook, Snapchat, Instagram, and other forms of social media. Many teenagers, youth and college students are asking questions on how they can escape loneliness, confusion and the unbelief that comes with hopelessness. I hope you can find an answer in this book.

Assumpta Onyinyechi Ude, Ph.D.
June 2019
Columbia, MD

ACKNOWLEDGMENTS

I gratefully acknowledge Dr. Veronica Amaku, Dr. Asopuru Okemgbo and my friend for life Dr. Oluwakemi Ogunsan for reviewing this book within a short notice. Thanks to Ms. Jane Uzuegbu for designing the cover concept page and Ms. Joycelyn Ogunsola, a successful author in her own rights for formatting, typesetting and facilitating the publication. My thanks to Chinonso Ude, Abisola, LaToya and Ewa for also picking up the manuscript to review at a very short notice.

I thank all the pastors of CAC Bethel Fellowship Church, Maryland as well as leaders and ministerial board members of Bethel Campus Fellowship and other members of the household of faith for fostering my daily renewal of hope in Christ. I am grateful to Professor and Dr. (Mrs.) Polycarp and Peace Nwoha, Dr. Sade Adejayan-Oluodojutimi, 'Daddy' Joe Alla, The Obiajunwas, Irohas, Ettus and Dr. & Dr (Mrs.) Cosmas Ilechukwu of Charismatic Renewal Ministries for their guidance and counsel while I tried to figure out life as a college student at the University of Ife. I acknowledge my friend, husband, and the Love of my life, Professor George Ude for his selfless and passionate love for the gospel that fueled this book. My Alleluia belongs to God and all praise to Him for inspiring and gracing me with inner strength and favor that made the writing and publication of this book a reality.

INTRODUCTION

"Hope does not put us to shame, because God's love has been poured out into our hearts through the Holy Spirit, who has been given to us." (Roman 5:5 NIV)

Things in the past. Things yet unseen. Wishes and dreams that are yet to come true. All of my hopes and all of my plans. My heart and my hands are lifted to you Lord, I offer my life to you. Everything I have been through. Use it for your glory. Lord I offer my days to you. Lifting my praise to you. As a pleasing sacrifice. Lord, I offer you my life.
(Claire Cloninger, Claire D. Cloninger, Don Moen)

"For thou art my hope (tikvah in Hebrew), O Lord GOD: thou art my trust from my youth." (Psalm 71:5). The literal English meaning of hope connotes an abstract feeling or longing, with anticipation that a good thing will happen. However, the Hebrew meaning of hope refers to an assured expectation of obtaining what one desires. An arbitrary desire for something without trust and faith in God is a vain illusion.

In Psalm 62:10, King David admonished us not to trust or put vain hope in stolen goods. There is a more certain and confident assurance that one's expectation will actualize when the attending trust, and faith is divinely rooted in Christ. Paul of Tarsus affirmed as an apostle of Christ Jesus by the command of God, that Christ is our hope of glory, and true hope comes with a divine encounter, not just a desire (1st Timothy 1:1; Colossians 1:27). Therefore, I invite you to join me and explore the paradox of real hope emerging from moments of despair.

There are several possible triggers of despair in this broken world. From fractured family, community and other relationships, to unrealized wishes and dreams. Hopelessness also occurs because of failed marriages, infertility, lack of career or educational attainment, reckless living, misplaced priorities, inability to break an addiction, academic or business failures.

Despondent feelings can creep in when a family member or loved one becomes prodigal and rebellious, or when one feels betrayed by trusted colleagues, friends, or family. Some become extremely discouraged after a protracted terminal illness, failing health, tragic accidents, or the loss of a loved one. For others, financial insecurity, sexual/mental/spousal abuse and other family dysfunctional events create uncertainties and mount undue pressure on them at some point in their lives. Regardless of the cause of the hopeless feelings, depression can culminate in suicidal or homicidal thoughts.

Sometimes, without adequate mentoring, spiritual and social support, hopelessness renders people negative and bitter. Loss of hope makes some people alienate themselves from friends, families and loved ones. Some people idolize their career and other mundane pursuits to escape from the crushing pain of despair. Others may resort to habitual outbursts of frustration and anger.

Some in their quest for help stumbled upon the Bible; they believed and embraced the truth in God's word that turned their hopeless experiences into nuggets of encouragement and restoration for others. For a person who encounters true hope in Christ, sad, depressing, traumatic events become divine opportunities to pause, reflect and surrender effortlessly to God, the Master Intelligent Designer. As the songwriter says, it becomes "so sweet to trust in Jesus" by letting the sovereignty of God play out in circumstances that challenge one's faith in God.

I desire that anyone in despair whose future appears dark will find hope through the unfolding of the narratives in this book. I also admire those who will dare to embrace Christ in their uplifting detour that can in retrospect; make their sad experience a pipeline of unending confidence. Now, catch your breath, tune in and come with me on this inspiring journey.

Chapter 1
When the Unexpected Happens

—

"For everything that was written in the past was written to teach us, so that through the endurance taught in the Scriptures and the encouragement they provide we might have hope." (Romans 15:4)

I'm trading my sorrow
I'm trading my shame
I'm laying them down
For the joy of the Lord
(Darrell Evans)

For many, the early years of life were the most spiritually awkward times of life. In these pre-teen and teen years, the battle for identity and eagerness to be visible if not managed well could lead to identity confusion, anxiety, depression and many other behavioral challenges prevalent in today's society. Youths are vulnerable to hopelessness, especially when the unexpected happens. Adults that are going through frustrating moments could also become very hopeless when the unexpected happens. Great legends, scholars, inventors, including authors of best sellers and those who had made popular news headlines had tragic endings because they became depressed, withdrawn and bitter while facing unanticipated situations. At such moments, some in their helplessness may turn to drugs, illicit sex, and alcoholism, while others in their dilemma vacillate between believing in either the true God or their imaginations.

The statistics on the outcomes of hopelessness paint a sad image of our modern society with disheartening conversations and postings on social media that transmit various musical signals in their subconscious. For an average schoolchild, bullies, peer pressure, and crushes are part of daily struggles that often trigger their choosing to follow their instincts or depend on God to navigate the terrain. At times, these painful life experiences make youth to seek answers to the questions that parade their minds and wrong guess in their move to prove their resilience may land them on crossroads. They may choose to reject their inner divine nudging, or subscribe to the voice that beckons them to seek abstract philosophical ideologies. The weariness and apathy of the soul sets in when believing in yourself, other relationships, and life pursuits are no longer able to fill a void that despair and depression breeds. Especially when there is no full assurance of hope and purpose in your world (Ephesians 2:12).

Are you familiar with the feelings of frustration that dawn when the unexpected happens? Have you imagined narrow escapes from other life shaking events and unexpected mishaps? Such was the sad experience of many including my parents that experienced the Civil War in Nigeria that generated fear, poverty, dangers, and uncertainties. In my parents' narrative of my infant-toddler years, they had several close shaves with death as the "air raid" (the airplane that fires gunshots or throws bombs) came very close to them in the marketplace. They lived in fear and faced the threat of death, day and night with the thundering sound of warplanes that drove them into constant hiding. They hid their firstborn infant while praying earnestly to God for protection.

My father's narrative in his script:

"I remember your mother and me "running" from one village, city or town to another. A bunker was a camouflaged underground shelter and people sought refuge in bunkers or under trees during air raids."

Who would have thought God still had a plan to preserve? Who could have saved me from the bomber plane that came so close, but God? Who could convince any parent that this child will survive? The sovereign God that worked behind the scenes was aware of my today that was not in the picture then.

As the first child and only girl with three siblings, then, I desperately desired a baby sister. You could not imagine my excitement when I heard the news of my Mother putting to bed a baby girl. Oh my world, what a moment! However, a bittersweet one as my mother had paralysis of her waist down her two legs following the delivery of my sister. While receiving traditional chiropractic care after the modern hospital system gave up on my mother, the unexpected happened—my little Sister Okechi took ill and died. I lost my only baby sister at about five weeks following her birth to pneumonia. In one minute, I was overjoyed at the birth of my baby sister and the next minute, the sibling that I cherished so much was no longer a living reality. I felt disappointed and sad. though amazed as I observed on the same day my sister passed that my mother miraculously stood on her feet and started walking independently after weeks of being bed-ridden.

I had so many questions that I could not ask anyone. I could not fathom why God spared my mother's life and allowed my little sister to die at five weeks of age. Have you questioned and wondered why God allows bad things to happen to good people? Perhaps you are dealing with sadness, difficulty, trauma from a loss of a friend or family member and other loved ones that have preceded you in death. Do not mourn any longer as one without true hope. Elizabeth Seton rightly said, *"Faith lifts a staggering soul on one side as hope supports it on* the other." Are you sorrowful, and bitter towards God because of disappointments and broken promises from unexpected sources? The next pages of your life are not yet in print. When the unexpected happens, you need God's help to choose following Christ rather than questioning Him.

C.S. Lewis once said, *"Sadness, death, sorrow, and pain of 'winter' does not have to leave us in a permanent hopeless mode."* After experiencing loss of his mother at an early age and abuse by a schoolteacher, Lewis admonished through his many books including 'A Grief Observed' on embracing true hope. Lewis said, *"Sometimes when the sadness cuts deep you need to look beyond the moment and look further refusing to be overwhelmed and know that there is more, there is hope."* Where else will you find hope in times of despair? Drinking, drugs, the club? The hope of Glory does not disappoint because it guarantees you of the unchanging love of God (Psalm 146:3-6). Lay down those burdens on the Rock of Ages, who is the shield, and shelter in the storms of loss.

Chapter 2
Times of Despair

—

"Praise the Lord God is thinking about me
Praise the Lord he has my name on his palm
Now my life is worth a living
I can face tomorrow
For I know God is thinking about me."
(Author Unknown)

Truly, hope does not exist outside of the reality of despair. If there is breath in our lungs and a beat in our hearts, times of despair are inevitable. Here comes my Mother's account on how the journey began:

Five months pregnant, went to a missionary clinic in Mile Four Abakaliki in the present Ebonyi state of Nigeria. After receiving an injection during the clinic visit, what was supposed to be an antenatal check-up turned into a high fever, bleeding, and obvious symptoms of miscarriage that threatened my life and survival as a fetus. The hope of full-term birth became very questionable as after a miraculous recovery from the bleeding, the civil war was looming, and Mother had to return home seven months pregnant.

My Father's narrative as written: *"On 20th Feb. 1968, a year after the wedding and shortly after the onset of the civil war in Nigeria, a bouncing baby girl—Onyinyechi was born in good health. As the Nigerian-Biafra War continued spreading, things were turning upside down with many people becoming refugees in their country. Church buildings, schools and market shops became beehives of refugees. Diseases of all kinds sprang up and getting food to eat was hard.*

Warplanes bombed here and there with people deserting their homes, land troops occupied the evacuated places killing people at night and looting goods and properties" Onyinyechi means "God's gift "while her Christian name, Assumpta, reminded me daily of a Rev. Sister, a kind physician with whom I worked in a hospital somewhere. That induced her parents to agree to her choice of reading Nursing. The success is clear, real, vivid and loud. Her careful and painstaking mother nursed her and as she was the first issue, her father did not want any baby nurse. Her painstaking mother devoted time to caring for her, making sure that her feeding, bathing and covering were very well received with attention. Shortly, her mother started teaching her to hold with her right-hand objects like her toys, the breast she sucks and her feeding bottles. Calling of 'Mama' and 'Papa' was taught also and before two-years of age, she could shout "Papa", "Mama", "water", "bread", and "egg."

Her father, a teacher, helped in showing her to draw objects on the wall such as bottles, bags, human heads, feet, pots and so on. Oral speech in Igbo and English such as 'Bia'-come, Go- 'pua', and run were included. Writing with chalk on the wall the alphabets and numbers and reading them with her mother's aid was a regular practice.

She was taught writing with pencils in exercise books, the primary one arithmetic and how to greet people in Igbo and English. At five, she was sent to school."

My early elementary school years came along with one of the most shocking events that shook my trust in communal life. I took the entrance examination to federal secondary (high) school with hope to attend one of my favorite schools at that time. Lo and behold, that desire did not become a reality. I felt devastated then because I was suddenly informed of pressing financial priority that would mean not proceeding to the school I desired to attend. It was a shattered dream. I had to forfeit that opportunity to attend a highly rated federal government high school at the time because of my parents' selfless offer to meet an extended family need. I felt very disappointed and unfulfilled as I continued to dream and wished I attended the school of my dream.

I struggled to study in a village high school setting that lacked adequate staffing for science teachers. The stories of *Girls Rising*, a global campaign for educating and empowering girls got me emotional as I could relate with children that could be wasting on our streets because of lost opportunity or lack of resource to help them pursue their life ambitions. I wonder their resentment and the hopeless feelings. In such times of despair, you need shoulders to stand on and a hand to hold you while you step into the seemingly unknown.

Growing up as a teenager and embracing the negative and pleasant surprises that life and people bring to the table began to take a toll on my perspectives and philosophy. I tried to peep into the future, wondering and imagining how life would be having unfulfilled dreams. I had so many unanswered questions about people, kinship, and living a communal life without fear. It was a struggle to expect or foresee brighter days in a community of harassments, negativity and bullying.

The struggle becomes real when those you seem to look up to could offer no assurance of protection and security due to their helpless condition. Life comes with both sad and sweet moments. Jesus wept when he heard the sad news of the death of his friend (John 11:35).

You may feel downcast and very discouraged when facing similar life events. Do not forget that those sad, hopeless moments are passing seasons in life.

May you never forget that Christ also experienced grief because of people's unfairness during His ministry on earth? (Mark 3:5). In your time of discouragement when it seems like Jesus is not coming through, you could as ask rhetorically as John did as he anticipated execution while in prison, *"Are you the Messiah we've been expecting, or should we keep looking for someone else?"* (Matthew 11:3).

Times of discouragement could progress into apathy where you lose the ability and excitement to dream for the future. You get unusually anxious and fearful, feel insecure and lose confidence in God, in yourself, and in others. The nights are filled with nightmares and weird dreams. You need a glimpse of hope at this time as it is impossible as often said to live a second without hope. The greatest gift the Bible gave to humanity is hope. It is important to fill yourself with the energizing and encouraging stories from real people with real issues that speak to contemporary issues of life. Do not be a lone ranger. In your times of despair go to Christ whose arms are always open waiting to make intercession for you. *"Therefore he is able to save completely those who come to God through him, because he always lives to intercede for them."* (Hebrews 7:25).

The bad news is that pain is an inevitable part of life. The good news is that you do not have to waste your pain and tears. You can invest and channel them to serve God's pre-ordained purpose. Connect with God's people. Many genuine Christians are out there to support you. Prepare to embrace your moments of despair with a fortitude from the Holy Spirit, our true Comforter, Strengthener and Advocate (John 14:26).

Chapter 3
Get Up

—

"The angel of the LORD came back a second time and touched him and said, "Get up and eat, for the journey is too much for you." (1st Kings 19:7)

For the praises of man I will never ever stand
To the kingdoms of this world, I'll never give
my heart away or shout my praise my allegiance and devotion, my heart's desire and
all emotion go to serve the man who died upon that tree only a God like you can be
worthy of my praise and all my hope and faith to only a king of all kings
Will I bow my knee and sing give my everything
(Tommy Walker)

As you have probably noticed by now, the first few years of my life were a mix-up of gallops and not-so-pleasant detours. At nine years of age, due to some strange extended family incidents, I began a journey filled with bittersweet moments that progressed quickly to swirling chaos. Your detours may not be extended family 'drama', yours may be difficult circumstances of poverty, not knowing where the next meal, school tuition or money to pay bills will come from. You may be on the road of being victimized and downtrodden by others you trusted and left with no chance of thriving, surviving or living.

As a student nurse at the age of 17, I started providing 'end of life care' or 'last office' which is the care a nurse has to provide to the body of a dead person shortly after the person has been officially pronounced by a physician. In my 15 years as a bedside nurse caring for people of all ages, I was amazed at how some of my patients exuded so much joy and possessed within them a deep serenity on their dying beds. I wondered about their courage and calm in spite of their battle with cancer, and other debilitating illnesses. I had to ask some of my dying patients that I developed a rapport with after being their caregiver for a while. When death was imminent the patients that identified as believers in Christ effortlessly exhibited behavior that showed that in their intuitive radar resonates, the fact that to die was gain (Philippians 1:21). I still sing a worship song that one of my patients at the University of Ife Teaching Hospital in Nigeria taught me in 1991 while she was dying.

My Jesus I love You, I love You
You are the world to Me, the world to me
If all *in this life shall fail, In life shall fail*
I put my hope in thee, my hope in thee
And when I will see your face
I will say Jesus I love thee

As the journey took me to the early adult years, such life experiences inspired me and reinforced my desire to seek what those patients I nursed that were dying with hope had in common. At 20 years of age, it dawned on me that I needed no other argument, as my faith could not find a resting place in a religious creed. God directed my footsteps. At a call to serve Christ made in Mozambique Hall during a student-led Sister's Fellowship Devotion at the former University of Ife, I stepped out of religion, unbelief, argument, self-pity, blaming others and embraced total faith in Christ. In my helpless estate, I surrendered my will to Christ the Master Designer, the Way Maker. He has promised to be by my side. He will not allow me to experience trials that I could not handle but has pledged to show me the escape route from any challenge (1 Corinthians 10:13).

As you take on this hope journey with me, check in with the inspiring lives of missionaries like Gladys and Esther Staines, Mary Slessor and Marie Durand. Including Jim Elliot whose inspirational quotes revealed the secret of his resolve and commitment to people who did not believe in His God. As he said, *"The man who will not act until he knows all will never act at all; He is no fool who gives what he cannot keep gaining what he cannot lose."* Therefore, I admonish you to rise up!

Do not be downcast. Do you know Ms. Hagar? (Genesis 16:1). A single mother who found herself in an ugly circumstance where she felt rejected after she was driven away by Sarah and Abraham. Sarah treated Hagar "harshly" (Genesis 16:6) and Hagar left Abraham's abusive and hostile home environment for the wilderness. She found hope in The El Roi—"The God Who Sees Me." (Genesis 16:13). A revelation God gave to Hagar after He saved her and her son Ishmael from death. God pursued her. That is so amazing of our God. There is no hopelessness in His agenda for you. What seemingly appears to be the end may actually be a stepping-stone for a glorious future. That is why C.H. Spurgeon in an attempt to express his experience of God said, *"The highest science, the loftiest speculation, the mightiest philosophy, which can ever engage the attention of a child of God is the name, nature, person, work, doing, the existence of the great God whom he calls his Father."* Jesus is a restorer of hope. *"Sir,"* the sick man answered, *"I have no one to help me into the pool when the water is stirred. While I am trying to get in, someone else goes down ahead of me."* Then Jesus said to him, *"Get up! Pick up your mat and walk."* (John 5:7-8). So, why are you despondent? Get up and walk! The Lord your God is with you and He will bring to pass whatever your heart desires that ultimately brings Him glory.

Chapter 4
The Synergy

—

"Praise be to God and Father of our Lord Jesus Christ, the Father of compassion and the God of all comfort, who comforts us in all our troubles so that we can comfort those in any trouble with the comfort we ourselves receive from God." (2nd Corinthians 1:3-4)

You made a way when our backs were against the wall,
And it looked as if it was over, You made a way
And we're standing here only because You made a way
And now we're here, looking back on where we come from
Because of You and nothing we've done, to deserve the love and mercy you've shown
But Your grace was strong enough to pick us up
(Travis Greene)

The word synergy as defined by Oxford Advanced Learner's Dictionary implies the creation of a whole or achievement of success by two or more people greater than the simple sum of people working on their own. The combined effect of facing depressing circumstances, and disappointments of life with faith in Christ, trust in the word of God and support from the household of faith could be far greater than living through inevitable depressing challenges of life in isolation and without Christ. You cannot fully appreciate the ingredients of lasting hope if you have never experienced disheartening moments of life. One would expect Christ Jesus to be joyful and happy when He heard about the death of Lazarus and knew He would raise him up. However, He wept (John 11:35).

Seasons of despair are disguised gifts from God that humbles us so that we do not become pompous, proud and arrogant. Therefore, the synergy occurs when by God's providence we trust and believe in God's word and encouragement from friends and family (Proverbs 27:17) despite our feelings. The synergy in despair and depression spiral down to hopelessness! However, synergy, in hope, is having a spirit of expectancy, anticipation, and faith to obtain what one desires in line with the word of God.

Are you facing opposition, especially from unexpected angles and it seems like there is no one else to lean on? Are you facing damaging criticism, opposition, and adversity perpetrated by others to achieve selfish agenda? Remember the Psalmist's journey and hold on those treasure tools hidden in God's word for overcoming the predicament of despair. Redirect your grievances to the real enemy of your destiny that has come to steal, kill and destroy your hope (John 10:10).

Times change and people change but when Christ remains your source of hope, He also orchestrates the faith that allows you to hope! What you hope for allows you to love; and works done in love are what makes your faith alive and practical. Does your pain drive you to Jesus or away from Him? Lorraine. E. Espenhain said, *"Many times in our lives, God throws us a curveball. How are we to respond so that we hit a home run, rather than strikeout"* Times of doubt will come. We may not necessarily escape some of life's tragedies. It is ironic that the words of encouragement from Apostle Paul were from letters he wrote while in prison anticipating execution (Philippians 4:4-8). For some who get so hurt by God's people and say, *"I am done with church"* because of their sad experiences within and outside the church, remember many of the followers of Christ did not escape the sword and fury of the adversaries of their time. In times like these, all you may need to do is to 'come out', confess and confide with a shepherd God has appointed over you and not be ashamed to be transparent and vulnerable.

"Blessed is the man who does not fall away on account of me." (Matthew 11:6). In times like these, some of your fellow believers like Job's friends may not even be very helpful and innocently wonder why you appear forsaken and like John the Baptist asked sincere but troubling questions, "Are you the One who was to come or should we expect someone else?" But as Jesus answered John's question, he told the disciples, "Jesus replied, "Go back and report to John what you hear and see. The blind receive sight, the lame walk, those who have leprosy are cleansed, the deaf hear the dead are raised, and the good news is proclaimed to the poor" (Matthew 11:4-5). Declare your faith, come out of hiding, and do not be ashamed because hope maketh one not ashamed. Remember your red seas, the former things and know that He is still in the business of making the glory of your later to shine brighter than your former. Come out from unbelief and march into victorious hope. After all, for you "to live is Christ and to die is gain" (Philippians 1:21).

Chapter 5
Confronting your Fears

—

Who shall separate us from the love of Christ? shall tribulation, or distress, or persecution, or famine, or nakedness, or peril, or sword? For I am persuaded, that neither death, nor life, nor angels, nor principalities, nor powers, nor things present, nor things to come, Nor height, nor depth, nor any other creature, shall be able to separate us from the love of God, which is in Christ Jesus our Lord.

(Romans 8:35, 38-39).

Christ is my rock, my refuge, my stronghold,
Firm as the tree's root that clutches the land.
He who has faith builds without worry,
not like the man who builds upon the sand.
I set my house on a solid foundation
Christ is my rock the root of my soul's recreation
(Author Unknown)

September 11, 2001 remains a sad day in American history. Out of that event, many beautiful things came forth including Matt Redman's song "Blessed Be Your Name". When you realize that pain and loss are inevitable in life, instead of getting too discouraged and despondent one needs to find true hope in God. Christ Jesus is able to turn one's ashes into beauty and help anyone to find something meaningful in a tragedy.

Every piece of art has a designer. Your life is not a mere cosmic chemical accident; you were well thought of, and uniquely made for a timeline and a unique purpose. Science, Technology, Arts and medical breakthroughs have given the sick a sense of hope by replacing ailing and failed body parts such as kidneys, hearts, and so on. However, many of these prosthetic body parts are artificial devices that could only function for a while. Psychotherapy may provide some temporary band-aid like relief from grief and emotional pain. However, no science or medical discovery has been able to replace or recreate a joyous soul or relieve the soul that is afflicted by despair, lack of fulfillment, or fear of the unknown.

It, therefore, stands to reason for one not to hold on broken cisterns but to accept the love God offers through Christ (Jeremiah 2:13). It takes undying confidence in Christ to proclaim beyond reasonable doubt that neither death, nor life, nor angels, nor principalities, nor powers, nor things present, nor things to come, nor height, nor depth, nor any other creature, shall be able to separate us from the love of God, which is in Christ Jesus our Lord (Romans 8:39).

Growing up as a teenager in Nigeria, though not a sportsperson, I cheered and admired my friends that played basket/netball, soccer, volleyball, and badminton. I was compelled to know some basics of football and basketball watching our boys in high school. However, Google became the 'go to' place. I read *'Baseball for Dummies'* to have a little understanding of baseball. I understand that a curve is a ball thrown by a right-handed pitcher that curves to the left of the pitcher or vice versa. The pitcher could predict and control the direction of the ball. However, the player that holds the bat does not know the exact course or direction the ball would take.

In some ways, I have been a caregiver to my Mother since 4th grade. Caring for aging loved ones requires sacrifice of one's time and energy; giving up social events, leisure and some appealing career opportunities. Attending to chores, multiple medical appointment visits could be too much for one to handle, especially in a setting where well-

meaning family and friends are too busy to provide helping hands. I worried, wondered and felt helpless. Thank God, for my church family, friends and Christian mentors that would pray and encourage me with the word of God. I also believe that the Holy Spirit Listened to my silent plea for help when no one was aware of my situation.
He saw my tears and sincere cry for rescue and one day I came across this scripture "But blessed is the one who trusts in the LORD, whose confidence is in him. He is like a tree planted by waters, that sends out its roots by the stream, and does not fear when heat comes, for its leaves remain green, and is not anxious in the year of drought, for it does not cease to bear fruit." (Jeremiah 17:7-8).

I realized that God could not allow trials that are heavier than I can handle but in every overwhelming situation as if I was in, provide a way of escape. I had no energy and needed wisdom, inspiration, and divine strength. I decided to hold onto God and consider whatever I thought was overwhelming responsibility and burnout as a ministry and instead of wishing this cup is taken from me, I learned to draw strength from His word with the understanding that if am in His will that He will supply sufficient grace to carry me through. I stopped focusing on others or myself and told myself "I am going to walk on the water." I moved my focus from the uncertainties and decided to place my trust daily in God's word knowing that He said I should not be weary in good doing because in due time He will reward me (Galatians 6:9).

Today, I greatly admire God, I marvel at the potency of His word, His understanding and wisdom is an anchor. God used all the seemingly challenging experience to build some resilience in me. God has caused all the detours, bends and potholes of the past decades to work out wonderful things in me. I am drawing strength from the Lord as my parents approach their twilight years and needing more attention and care. In the past twenty-five years, in spite of the enormous task involved in being the 'go to person' in caring for the old and young,

God spared my marriage, restored my health, and moved me to a fulfilling career path.

God has the final say. He is the master Architect, the one that holds the future that I once dreaded to see. Because He lives you can face tomorrow with a smile.

Chapter 6
The Way of Escape

–

"No temptation has overtaken you except what is common to mankind.
And God is faithful; he will not let you be tempted beyond what you can bear.
But when you are tempted, he will also provide a way out so that you can endure it."
(1st Corinthians 10:13)

This world could never satisfy, the longing in my soul
When all is lost and hope is dry when all I feel is cold
I'm coming back to Your presence
I'm coming back to Your presence
'Cause there's a hunger and a thirst
I am desperate, immerse me
I'm not waiting, not anymore
I need You, Lord, I need You, Lord
(David and Nicole Binion)

The Bible highlights some negative surprises of hope. Smart and analytical minds may wonder why the God of the Bible would allow David's child to die after he believed God to spare his life (2Samuel 12:14-24). Did God not say, *"Hope does not disappoint"*? David was not angry with God neither with his servant Nathan the Prophet. Rather he got up in surrendered thanksgiving that resulted in the birth of Solomon.

Have you ever felt wounded by God or by God's people? Does it leave you surprised or disappointed? Do you have times where you want to throw in the towel of your commitment to Christ? Emily Dickerson in one of her poems described hope as "*a feathered bird that is permanently perched in the soul of every human. There it sings, never stopping in its quest to inspire.*" Nothing else in my life, not a thing is able to offer me a permanent Hope outside Christ. That is why Frank M. Davis song, "Savior Lead Me" often resonates to my soul.

> "*Oh, to be without a Savior! With no hope or refuge nigh; Can it be, O blessed Savior, One without Thee dares to die!*"

No matter how we try to redefine quality of life, there is no quality to life without divine hope. Hal Lindsey said, *"Man can live for forty days without food, about three days without water, about eight minutes without air but only for one second without hope."* Sometimes you get confused, burnt out and at times want to drop the ball. Many today have taken the way of miserable and lonely life concealed in reckless living. Some hide their feelings and pretend all is well even though they feel life is pointless. As a result, they resort to latching onto their headphones, listening to dark music and watching music videos and movies that band-aids their pain, anger and despair. You lose nothing from gaining a Savior in Christ. Instead of wallowing in emptiness, walking away, behind or ahead of your Maker, like Joseph and Mary, you need to retrace your steps back to the Savior (Luke 2:41-51). Money, sex, drugs, power, work, material possession, relationships or even our ministries cannot offer us hope. Do not leave Him behind pursuing fame and glamour of 'ministry' The way of escape comes from looking intently into the perfect law that gives freedom and continuing in it...not forgetting what you have heard...but acting on it by believing it to be true (James 1: 25).

Chapter 7
The Irony of Failure

—

"For I know the thoughts that I think toward you, says the LORD, *thoughts of peace and not of evil, to give you a future and a hope." (Jeremiah 29:11)*

God of creation there at the start before the beginning of time.
With no point of reference, You spoke to the dark and fleshed out the wonder of light
And as You speak, a hundred billion galaxies are born in the vapor of Your breath the planets form.
If the stars were made to worship so will I can see Your heart in everything You've made.
Every burning star a signal fire of grace. If creation sings Your praises so will I, God of Your promise You don't speak in vain. No syllable empty or void. For once You have spoken All nature and science. Follow the sound of Your voice
And as You speak

As I narrated in a previous chapter, I did not have the privilege of attending a high school staffed with well-experienced science and math teachers. Yet, I knew I needed math and science to pursue my career of choice. Grace had it that I got admission into a 5-year baccalaureate program in Nursing despite my weak physics and math foundation. The program's course work was intense with combined curriculum for associate degree program in nursing, midwifery and public health nursing.

I took General Chemistry, Math, Physics and Experimental Physics with other biological science classes during my first year. I failed some of those science classes and spent an extra year in college.

The university almost dismissed me from the nursing program. It was a very heartbreaking experience, especially given my family's financial difficulty at that time.

I could not imagine how life had turned out that period as I was on a hold up overlooking the Niger River near Onitsha in Nigeria, thank God! On that fateful day, it was as if the songwriter echoed. God's unconditional love lifted me while I was sinking from many negative thoughts and restrained me from taking the next step. I had not learned to trust God in a disappointing situation and lacked the faith to believe I could continue as a student. That year I needed God on a personal level, or I was going to give up on life and myself. In my distress, I desired a relationship with Him. To the glory of God, my experience of failure led me to placing my trust and faith in Christ that transformed my perspective about failure.

The following year, I earned a University scholarship award as the best student in my class. I completed my program in six years that first seemed 'forever' when I had an extra year added to my 5-year course. I fell deeply in love with Jesus during those years; it was in this University that Christ saved me and I met the man that eventually became my husband. We married and he got admission to study in the United States, and here we are serving God, humanity, and raising a family.

Have you experienced any type of failure in your business, board exam, marriage or academics? Are you unable to start a family, get your dream job, have children, and make enough money to support yourselves? Like the songwriter, can you see God's hand in those mishaps? Do you see a future of hope beyond the moment? King David fell into sin, Peter denied Christ and other Bible characters that failed the test of their faith provide extra examples that failure is not fatal. What kills is, when due to pride, you refuse to repent genuinely, turn to God and follow the next steps that He instructs you to take

Chapter 8
When It Makes No Sense

—

"Therefore, since we have been justified through faith,
we have peace with God through our LORD Jesus Christ,
through whom we have gained access by faith into this grace
in which we now stand. And we boast in the hope of the glory of God.
Not only so, but we also glory in our sufferings, because we know that suffering
produces perseverance; perseverance, character; and character, hope.
And hope does not put us to shame, because God's love has been
poured out into our hearts through the Holy Spirit, who has been given to us."
(Romans 5:1-5)

What I see right now, doesn't look like what you promised
and the way I feel right now doesn't feel like what you said
All this fear and doubt doesn't look like what you promised
and the way I feel right now doesn't feel like what you said
But you cannot tell a lie
Oh no you cannot tell a lie
No you cannot tell a lie
All your promises are yes and amen
(Grace for Every Mountain-Passersby Project)

There have been times, as far as I was concerned, that a flicker of eternal hope of the Scriptures was all I needed to have compassion towards those who have hurt me because of my expression of faith in Christ. As a young convert and a professing born-again Christian, I forfeited my privileges and ridiculed by well-meaning loved ones. Somehow, I was not angry towards anyone. Rather I had peace and had an assurance that I did not experience when I did not have the Bible as my resource. The scriptures helped me to understand why embracing Christ could generate such controversy. Nevertheless, God allowed all of that humbling experience for a glorious future He was orchestrating.

I have learned not to question God when passing through trials and persecutions for living godly in Christ Jesus. A while ago, I read *"The Shack"*, a USA Today Bestseller that answered some of the life questions that many people had about hopelessness. In *"The Shack"*, William P. Young metaphorically addressed the hurt of being stuck in the feeling of anger and despair as we face sad events that we think we do not deserve. As I was writing this book, the Washington Post reported the Las Vegas shooting as the worst mass shooting in U.S History. CNN reported one of the worst global disasters in Zimbabwe and Mozambique. Every day, week and month Twitter, private conversations and News Headlines carry news of either gunman killings or shootings. In various parts of the world there are so many atrocities happening in developing countries that are under-report such as race riots and massacre, leaving individuals and families with bitterness and resentment and a growing generation battling with post-traumatic stress and depression.

We do not glory in the pain from this troubling news. We do not glory in a cruel world filled with callous people who have lost hope in God and express their bitterness towards God by promoting evil and injustice, where man has become self-centered and aims in being his own god. We glory in the real hope that out of the debris of these disasters will rise a new heaven and a new earth when destruction will cease, and man will lose the ability to hurt each other and the environment where God placed them. *"Then I saw "a new heaven and a new earth," for the first heaven and the first earth had passed away, and there was no longer any sea…. He will wipe every tear from their eyes."* (Revelation 21:1, 4).

Chapter 9
Keep on Keeping on

—

"He has delivered us from such a deadly peril, and he will deliver us again.
On him we have set our hope that he will continue to deliver us." (2nd Corinthians 1:10)

My hope is built on nothing less
Than Jesus' blood and righteousness
I care not trust the sweetest frame
But wholly trust in Jesus' Name
Christ alone; cornerstone
Weak made strong in the Savior's love
Through the storm,
He is Lord, Lord of all
(2011 Hill-song music)

Have you wondered why some are so blessed with a good job, beautiful houses, great academic and professional degrees, husband, wife, children, heavy bank account, estate and yet have no meaningful life of hope? Quest for the meaning of life has driven many into the fallacy of seeking power within themselves. In their emptiness searching for the fulfillment that does not come from discovering oneself but from trusting in God who had existed before their being.

The pressure of secularism, humanism, and new age dogma that claims that biblical truth is relative, and miracles are myths have left so many, *"running a hundred miles an hour in the wrong direction."* (*"Does Anybody Hear Her"* by Casting Crowns). Materialism and pursuit of religion and spirituality have also given some a false sense of confidence and have left others in a place of dilemma where they continue to compete and compare themselves with themselves but are not satisfied with their lives.

Are you satisfied? Are you content? Or are you looking at and mimicking your own definition of success and fame? Are you chasing others' ideas and visions?

Abraham had experienced God not just as a Supreme-Being but as a friend. *"But thou, Israel art my servant, Jacob whom I have chosen, the seed of Abraham my friend."* (Isaiah 41:8). Hence Abraham could count on the potency and efficacy of God's promise to him as it is written: *"I have made you the father of many nations. He is our Father in the sight of God, in whom He believed—the God who gives life to the dead and calls into being things that were not. Against all hope, Abraham, in hope believed and so became the father of many nations, just as it had been said to him, "So shall your offspring be."*(Romans 4: 17-18). If you know who you are, your purpose, where you are going, whose you are then you know that when all you have is hope you have everything that hope brings.

So many are hanging in there filled with regrets from their past. Perhaps in their efforts to discover themselves or in a quest for spirituality, fell victims of lies that claim that all obstacles and hopeless feelings are perceptions, not reality. Probably because they lacked exemplary godly mentors or cannot figure out a way out with their brain cells. The Holy Spirit of God provided the answer to my questions and clarified my curiosities as I explored His life as is written in the Bible.

The things that our visual senses and mind can process are temporal and the things that we cannot explain with our rational minds at times are immortal. Today as I celebrate decades of living hope, I testify that Christ is the cornerstone of my unshakable hope. Not because of my abilities or strength but this is due to the confident assurance of the truth of what He has done in the past and the present. *"He has delivered me from such a deadly peril, and he will deliver me again. On him, I have set my hope that he will continue to deliver me."* *(2 Cor. 1:10).*

Chapter 10
In Good Times and Bad Times

—

"Though the fig tree should not blossom and there be no fruit on the vines,
though the yield of the olive should fail and the fields produce no food."
Habakkuk 3:17-19

My faith has found a resting place, Not in device nor creed;
I trust the Ever living One, His wounds for me shall plead.
Enough for me that Jesus saves, This ends my fear and doubt;
A sinful soul I come to Him, He'll never cast me out
.I need no other argument, I need no other plea;
It is enough that Jesus died, And that He died for me.
My heart is leaning on the Word,The written Word of God,
Salvation by my Savior's name,Salvation through His blood.
I need no other argument, I need no other plea
;it is enough that Jesus died, And that He died for me.
On Christ the solid Rock I stand all other ground is sinking sand,
All other ground is sinking sand.
I need no other argument, I need no other plea; it is enough that Jesus died,
And that He died for me
(Carol Ann McClure / Brendan McKinney)

As a long-term caregiver since age 9, I have had a little share of what it means for the pain to take all of one's energy and leave no single space for hope. I applaud the home where the practice and tenets of religion were birthed and I'm grateful for a mother who laid the foundational stones of my knowledge of God. However, religion without the anchor of the scriptures and a transforming experience of salvation in Christ as a backup only birthed self-righteousness and hypocrisy. Mere religious observances had an appearance of wisdom, with their self-imposed worship, their false humility and their harsh treatment of the body but lacked any value in restraining my sensual indulgence. (Colossian 2:23). Religion without having an understanding of the saving love of the blessed Trinity could not take me above impure thoughts and beyond moments when self-will and determination failed. When you are born and raised in a religious home, you naturally become acquainted with religious life.

The danger of religion is that it does not give a chance to see your faith as part of daily practical life. Sadly, professing a personal faith in Christ as one's savior and calling the God of the Bible a Father makes one a social outcast. Now things are getting better in some parts of the world, while in some other parts things are getting worse. In some parts of the world, Christians are losing their lives, their usual support system because of their desire and allegiance for Christ and considered a fanatic and a lunatic. How could you have left the stoic, fashionable, popular traditional church to join the so-called *"mushroom church"*? You have messed up the pride of the family. Ironically, in spite of losing the succor that comes from family and acquaintances, a peace settled with knowing Christ the Lover of my soul and the one that lifted the burden of my sins.

My fear of death was broken in an instant when I yielded all personal struggles to Christ, including the efforts to please others. I realized that the battle was over and that it is Christ that is coming to live out His life through me effortlessly, all the work I need to do is not corporal works of mercy. Christ finished the work of saving me from sorrows, sickness, sin, and despair on the Cross. The only 'work' I need to do is believe in the finished work and accept the package for abundant life reserved for me here and in eternity (John 6:29).

I had a full assurance of hope. The future was bright because of the Son, I could literally fly, Wow! My confidence was sky high and even beyond because I am no longer a slave to sin; no longer a banished daughter of Eve. I am in Christ Jesus and am now Abraham's seed, therefore—an heir to the promise. Yes, my faith has found a resting place, no more in religious device nor creed.

I need no other agreement, I need no other pleas, it is enough that Jesus died and that He died for me. *"Even youths grow tired and weary, and young men stumble and fall; But those who hope in the Lord will renew their strength. They will soar on wings like eagles; they will run and not grow weary; they will walk and not be faint."* (Isaiah 40:30-31).

I discovered the Bible after my decision to accept Christ is teaching, tasted of His goodness and potency of His word and that event transformed my life until today. I discovered that the Bible addressed daily issues of life. I have found it a useful and practical template for handling life challenges, failures and success. It has equipped me to deal with uncertainties in life and to interact better with people from different walks of life. The decision to make Christ's teaching as a standard has helped me to develop a positive attitude. It has been a helpful mental health resource for me as well.

Humans do not metamorphose into 'spiritual giants'. As Tony Evans rightly stated *"God implants spiritual seed into the soul of the sinner. "*In John 3:3 Jesus told Nicodemus *"Very truly I tell you, no one can see the kingdom of God unless they are born again."* In order to receive this *"spiritual seed"* Nicodemus wondered if someone had to enter a second time into their mother's womb to be born. Jesus went further and explained the process that, *"no one can enter the kingdom of God unless they are born of water and the Spirit. Flesh gives birth to flesh, but the Spirit gives birth to spirit."* A man born of a woman must believe in something. With the second birth, we receive a new life when we place our faith in Jesus Christ. As Paul stated, we become saved new creatures in Christ (2Corinthians 5:17, John 17:3) exclusively done by the Holy Spirit with the yielding of man's spirit. When we hear and accept God's word of hope in our heart—the Spirit mixes with the Word and new life begins automatically.

It is a real-life experience that comes with thirst and hunger for the infilling of the Holy Spirit and desires for the sincere milk of the word (1Peter 2:2). The continued hearing of the word of God, through regular communion with God's people, facilitate maturity in handling life challenges that breed despair. We have to eat the right and balanced diet. Therefore, it matters where we attend church and the teachings that we embrace at this early stage.

The quality of the word you receive will determine how your spirit and your old unregenerate flesh/self continually reacts to the pressures of stress and distress. As you taste of God's unfailing encouragement through His word, you will begin to desire what God loves. You will want to dig deeper and begin to chew the meat and bones of the word of God. The Holy Spirit continues His awesome work of watering by the word and enable you to dominate the old 'you.' That is why Paul admonished us to be filled with the Holy Spirit (Ephesians 5:18). Being filled with the Holy Spirit should be an intentional daily action of a Christian. This daily habit enables the new you to grow and override the old you. The new growing seed inside of you makes your old self that craves after the world and its attractions uncomfortable. Your old spiritual appetite is lost, and your moral mechanism becomes re-aligned as that seed grows. Unlike the work of re-birth, this process does not happen automatically, it requires effort and willingness to be like Christ, which is the ultimate goal.

What makes trusting God so sweet is that *"He has given us his very great and precious promises, so that through them you may participate in the divine nature, having escaped the corruption in the world caused by evil desires. For this very reason, make every effort to add to your faith goodness; and to goodness, knowledge; and to knowledge, self-control; and to self-control, perseverance; and to perseverance, godliness; and to godliness, mutual affection; and to mutual affection, love. For if you possess these qualities in increasing measure, they will keep you from being ineffective and unproductive in your knowledge of our Lord Jesus Christ. But whoever does not have them is nearsighted and blind, forgetting that they have been cleansed from their past sins. Therefore, my brothers and sisters make every effort to confirm your calling and election. For if you do these things, you will never stumble."* 2 Peter 1:4-10.

Chapter 11
The Rose in the Thorn

—

"Remember that at that time you were separate from Christ,
excluded from citizenship in Israel and foreigners to the covenants of the promise,
without hope and without God in the world." (Ephesians 2:12)

My only hope is you, Jesus. My only hope is you,
From early in the morning to late at night,
My only hope is you. My only peace is you, Jesus
My only peace is you, from early in the morning to late at night, my only peace is
you. My only joy is you, Jesus, My only joy is you, from early in the
morning to late at night, my only joy is you. All that I need is you, Jesus
All that I need is you, from early in the morning to late at night, all that I need is you.
My only hope is you, Jesus my only hope is you, from early in the morning to late at
night, my only hope is you. From early in the morning to late at night, my hope is you
(John Paul Trimble)

My decision to place my faith in Christ and accept the Bible as
my life manual has had a profound impact on how I handle life
challenges. In fact, all things especially hopeless experiences of life
have ultimately worked for my good. When I had the diagnosis of
Hypertension at what I considered early in life, I was numb and very
discouraged. Especially seeing the route this disease has taken my
mother. Hope always leaves a footmark for the future. One of those
footmarks traces to an organization born from a place of reaching out to

a place of giving back. I recall with gratitude to God creating a forum that advocates for cardiovascular disease prevention in women resulted from my experience living with the diagnosis. Today, I share a message of hope to the sick and ailing through various health services. Few of the beautiful roses that I picked from those thorns of sad medical reports. Interestingly enough, I thought of leaving this rose ever fresh for the future when I decided to dedicate my Ph.D. dissertation to studying hypertension in West-African-born women. Like Tony Evans said, *"God cannot mold and shape our lives unless we're willing to surrender and be transparent before Him"*.

The diagnosis of hypertension is a label that I have acknowledged the receipt but refused to wear it as an outfit. I rather, use it as a tool for promoting local and global community wellbeing. Hypertension is no more a crutch of inborn disease. It has become part of my resource kit for equipping people living with chronic illness with true and lasting hope.

Chapter 12
You Need an Anchor

—

"We have this hope as an anchor for the soul, firm and secure." Hebrews 6:19

We have an anchor that keeps the soul
Steadfast and sure while the billows roll,
Fastened to the Rock which cannot move,
Grounded firm and deep in the Savior's love.
We have an anchor that keeps the soul
Steadfast and sure while the billows roll,
Fastened to the Rock which cannot move,
Grounded firm and deep in the Savior's love.
Will your anchor hold in the storms of life,
When the clouds unfold their wings of strife?
When the strong tides lift, and the cables strain,
Will your anchor drift or firm remain?
We have an anchor that keeps the soul
Steadfast and sure while the billows roll,
Fastened to the Rock which cannot move,
Grounded firm and deep in the Savior's love
(Robin Mark)

Depression, despair, and hopelessness are a vicious cycle that feeds on each other, and psychologists as helpful as they are will counsel you to focus on inspiration and support. But how do you maintain hope when you are in a relationship with an inspirational person that is unavailable or inaccessible? That is why you need to embrace true hope and faith in Christ, the never-forsaking God who assured us of His EVER presence as an anchor (Hebrews 13:5).

According to Webster's Dictionary, an anchor is a heavy device that is attached to a boat or ship by a rope or chain and that is thrown into the water to hold the boat or ship in place and prevent it from floating away. It is used to stabilize a ship or boat in heavy weather, storms, and waves of the sea to prevent it from sinking. Hope is an anchor for the soul. There are times one may not find any logical or human reason to expect something good to happen. Maybe not accomplishing your dream, or breaking unhealthy stubborn habits, delay in marriage, attaining a job promotion, or childbirth. Whatever it is, please stop drifting in despair, put your anchor back down. Shift your focus from circumstances, people, friends, family, pastors, career, and certificates and begin to look unto Christ the Promise Keeper.

Joseph, one of Jacob's children, was in a place where he could have easily committed suicide. He was falsely accused by his own brothers, betrayed and forgotten inside the pit and prison. He must have wondered about his dream and vision. Moses was in a similar situation when in front of him was the red sea, beside him was the angry people he was supposed to be leading, and behind him was an army ready to annihilate them. The fact that there is a delay does not mean there is a denial. Worrying and self-pity will be drifting but keep your anchor down.

Chapter 13
No Expiration

—

"If our hope in Christ is for this life alone we are of all people most to be pitied."
(1st Cor. 15:19)

Because He lives, I can face tomorrow
Because He lives all fear is gone
Because I know He owns my future
And life is worth a living just because He lives
(Bill Gaither)

We are living in a time when the world is desperately in need of real hope. Man has devised new ways of perpetrating evil, lawlessness, and wickedness with politically correct nomenclature. It is scary but not new under the sun. That is why a life without hope in Christ is something that needs consideration. I am not sure if there is any human being that lived till the age of awareness that did not wonder about what happens after death. Including those who never imagined losing the privilege of a burial and a tombstone erected in their honor. Have you wondered why your nightmares and exciting dreams while asleep turn to reality when you wake up noticing a remnant of the tears of joy or torments? Have you ever been able to wake up to say, *"Thank God it was just a dream"*? If so you do not need a divine encounter or believe in the Divine to know that there is life beyond death. Unlike other created things like animals, hope, faith, and love are the soulish-spiritual nature humans share with God.

When you sleep your body and soul go into sleep, but your spirit is awake and if you sleep on or transition to eternity your mortal body gives way to your spirit that now sleeps into an eternal miserable or happy state. Death is a part of the journey to eternity but those who believe in the only King that conquered death have hope of life beyond the grave. Because He lives you also shall live. *"Before long, the world will not see me anymore, but you will see me. Because I live, you also will live."* (John 14:19). He is the resurrection and the life (John 11:25). *"The one who believes in me will live even though they die."* (John 19:21-30).

Alleluia! Our hope does not expire when our body expires. If only for this life we have hope in Christ, we are of all people most to be pitied (I Corinthians 15:9). A believer's absence in the body means present with the Lord. *"For we know that if the earthly tent we live in is destroyed, we have a building from God, an eternal house in heaven, not built by human hands. Meanwhile we groan, longing to be clothed instead with our heavenly dwelling, because when we are clothed, we will not be found naked. 4 For while we are in this tent, we groan and are burdened, because we do not wish to be unclothed but to be clothed instead with our heavenly dwelling, so that what is mortal may be swallowed up by life. 5 Now the one who has fashioned us for this very purpose is God, who has given us the Spirit as a deposit, guaranteeing what is to come. Therefore, we are always confident and know that as long as we are at home in the body we are away from the Lord."* (2Corinthians 5:1-6).

Child of God, your hope in Christ does not expire because His love will not let you go and is stronger than death because Christ willingly died and defeated the power of death. "No one can have greater love than to give his life for his friends." (John 15:13).

"Blessed be the God and Father of our Lord Jesus Christ! *"According to his great mercy, he has caused us to be born again to a living hope through the resurrection of Jesus Christ from the dead, to an inheritance that is imperishable, undefiled, and unfading, kept in heaven for you, who by God's power are being guarded through faith for salvation ready to be revealed in the last time. In this you rejoice, though now for a little while, if necessary, you have been grieved by various trials, so that the tested genuineness of your faith—more precious than gold that perishes, though it is tested by fire—may be found to result in praise and glory and honor at the revelation of Jesus Christ."* (1 Peter 1:3-6).

"So we do not lose heart. Though our outer self is wasting away, our inner self is being renewed day by day. For this light momentary affliction is preparing for us an eternal weight of glory beyond all comparison, as we look not to the things that are seen but to the things that are unseen. For the things that are seen are transient, but the things that are unseen are eternal." (2 Corinthians 4:16-18)

Chapter 14
Sing with Me

—

"Sing to the Lord a new song, his praise in the assembly of his faithful people.
Let Israel rejoice in their Maker; let the people of Zion be glad in their King.
Let them praise his name with dancing and make music to him with timbrel and harp.
For the Lord takes delight in his people; he crowns the humble with victory.
Let his faithful people rejoice in this honor and sing for joy on their beds.
May the praise of God be in their mouths and a double-edged sword in their hands,
to inflict vengeance on the nations and punishment on the peoples,
to bind their kings with fetters, their nobles with shackles of iron,
to carry out the sentence written against them—
this is the glory of all his faithful people." (Psalm 149)

Praise the Lord.
Praise the Lord God is thinking about me
Praise the Lord he has my name on his palm
Now my life is worth a living
I can face tomorrow
For I know God is thinking about me
Author-Unknown

The weapon of praise in combating hopelessness is profound. That is why even science invented music and talk therapy. I have found worship as a powerful tool for enjoying life in the midst of storms. Christ promised I will never leave you nor forsake you. I will go with you (Exodus 33:14). One day I read a poem that got me thinking and asking myself about what will ultimately mean so much to me in the next 30 years of my life.

Life is a journey, a long one for many and a short one for some depending on one's perspective. From the time you can nurse feelings of fear, anger, guilt, and despair, you begin to see the need for someone to lean on. In addition, some responsibilities set an expectation on you and somehow you become accountable to colleagues, bosses, neighbors, classmates, and various families you become part of. Whether you are a student, working professional, father, mother, wife, husband, daughter, son, sister, brother, friend, minister, church worker, leader, daughter or son in law; pretty soon you find out that juggling life expectations can be very frustrating if you have no real hope. Your relationship with Christ fuels the vehicle of your mind for the journey of life but know that God is beside you and with you in your purpose and calling, and where and how God has called you to serve. Paul realized this and that helped him to focus on his purpose—sent to the gentiles. Peter also discovered his purpose—sent to the Jews.

Jesus' reason for enduring the journey from Bethlehem to Calvary was because He was sent to the lost and to die as a ransom for all humanity. The certainty of hope as promised by God provides us with a tangible end that one can visualize with the eyes of faith and with a heart of trust. As you read through the last pages of this book in anticipation and expectancy, remember to switch from wishful thinking to the real hope in Christ that you can grasp. The Christian's hope is rooted in waiting. We wait for the blessed hope—*"the appearing of the glory of our great God and Savior, Jesus Christ."* (Titus 2:13). In the process of waiting on God to perform in reality what He has promised, we go through a series of feelings of impatience, anger, and doubt and blame shifting. Do not be discouraged when your human tendencies run contrary to the unchangeable word of God upon which every Christian should hinge his or her hope.

Real hope walks obediently with the Lord. *"Wait for the LORD; be strong and let your heart take courage; yes, wait for the LORD."* (Psalm 27:14). If you have become paralyzed by past disappointments, chaos, hurts or seemingly dashed wishes, take a moment now and resolve one more time, to hold onto this hope in Christ. I have been singing melodies of hope from moments of despair for the last three decades of my life and counting. Through these lessons, I have developed lyrics for trusting in Jesus more than when I first knew Him. Now sing with me:

- *At times, poverty is a path a person chooses.*
- *Do not wish you are someone else.*
- *Let God, rather than people reward you.*
- *Many of your fears are not real.*
- *Human beings are inherently selfish.*
- *There is so much to learn from anybody.*
- *Believing and living the bible leaves no regret.*
- *Be content with who you are while aspiring to be Christ-like.*
- *Do not be surprised: People change over time.*
- *There are many that you will help that will never appreciate you, keep helping anyway.*
- *Give and give-It will come back to you.*
- *There is hope in Christ.*
- *Childish faith prolongs life.*
- *The only debt that you will never finish paying is the debt of love.*
- *You cannot change anybody including yourself.*
- *Feelings are fleeting.*
- *No condition is permanent.*

- *Do not be carried away by the praise of man while you receive them with humility.*
- *You can never hear all that people say about you to focus on what God has said and is saying.*
- *Respect positions people occupy in your life when their personality puts you off*
- *Walls have ears be careful how you talk*
- *Be careful who you trust with your secrets*
- *Let go it's not worth the hassle*
- *Honorable marriage: Make the foundation godly strong*
- *Hard work pays off and pays long*
- *Vision prolongs life*
- *Hope keeps you running though fainting*
- *No graduation from the school of patience and perseverance*
- *God's grace and Mercy the only reason am not giving up*
- *Many things are created in the place of private prayer*
- *God is real and not just an imaginary Being*
- *The Bible is a book of life providing the template for living*
- *There is a friend that sticks closer than a brother*
- *Focusing early in life makes you an expert sooner than*
- *Experience teaches and is the best teacher*
- *Learn to listen more than you respond*
- *If you have to do it, then don't complain*
- *Wisdom is the greatest asset*
- *God will always make a way of escape*
- *There is a void only God can fill.*
- *Failure is an essential ingredient of a successful life-God has a final say.*
- *God's ways are not necessarily our ways*
- *Trials are God's pruning knife don't miss it*

- *Pick your battles and overlook what you cannot change*
- *Do not give pearls to swine–some people cannot handle the truth*
- *Favor is from the Lord let God fight for you*
- *Do not lean on your understanding*
- *Do not blow your trumpet of praise*
- *Learn to take time, pamper yourself and enjoy the fruit of your labor-Tomorrow is not promised*
- *The way to show off your leadership is to serve when no one is looking.*
- *Lower your expectations of people and heighten your anticipation from God and you shall have fewer surprises.*

Chapter 15
The Treasured Gifts of Hope

—

"When Joseph and Mary had done everything required by the Law of the Lord,
they returned to Galilee to their own town of Nazareth." (Luke 2:39)

"God sets the lonely in families,[as] he leads out the prisoners with singing;
but the rebellious live in a sun-scorched land." (Psalm 68:6).

The boundary lines have fallen for me in pleasant places; surely I have a delightful inheritance.
(Psalm 16:6).

I love this family of God
So closely knitted into one
You have taken me into your heart
And I'm so glad to be a part
Of this great family
(Author Unknown)

I had that 'A-HA' moment reflecting on the three scriptures that informed this chapter. David once forgotten, not included in the family picture of Jesse at a time and not even counted as part of his family, scorned, ridiculed and rejected at a time declared he had a delightful inheritance (Psalm 16:6). Though as a prophet he spoke concerning his messianic ancestry, he also realized he needed the love of a family in his lonely moments on earth (Psalms 68:6). I deeply treasure the nurturing I received from various families. I appreciate the gifts of God's family including priests, pastors, mentors and various men and women of God that have ministered to my life when I needed someone to look up to. I will fondly remember and appreciate Dr. Felix Okogbo (Professor of Medicine and Dean Faculty of Clinical Sciences, Ambrose Alli University, Ekpoma, Edo State, Nigeria) and Dr. (Mrs.) Felicia Okogbo of blessed memory who God used mightily as my destiny helpers during my six months of training at a local nursing diploma school in 1986. I owe my university education to their insistent wise counsel. They saw me today, many years ago. Today, our home has become to many college students the proverbial revolving door because Aunty Felicia welcomed me with open arms into her home anytime I needed a "retreat center;" during my short school breaks. Rest in Peace 'Godmother'.

I treasure the family—parents', siblings, husband, and children that have been part of the journey. At the stage of concluding this book, two days after my father surprisingly agreed to attend my graduation if given a visa he was rushed to the hospital after an acute stroke episode. According to doctor's report, his health has suddenly deteriorated. I believe it is another lesson on the synergy that occurs with trust and faith as I hope against hope knowing that God is able to quicken Papa's mortal body and make him well. If the inevitable becomes obvious, I am confident that God is with him and will not allow him to suffer in his twilight years. As it is written, and I believe that "Against all hope, Abraham in hope believed and so became the father of many nations, just as it had been said to him, *"So shall your offspring be."* (Romans 4:18). Therefore, in the remaining pages, I enumerate the treasures in the gifts of family starting with my father.

Papa, clearly, as far as I could recollect your family and community life has been rocky; then again, I have now learned that few parents are without challenges. Reflecting, as your first child it's not hard to say that our family has weathered storms of hostility from unexpected sources. There was a season we did not have enough to eat not necessarily, because we were poor. Though you fell short of many of my ideals, with my understanding of the scriptures and interacting with the world, those things have little, if any, hold on me now. Instead, I frequently recall the good times I had with you. Papa, though I grew up hearing your threats of divorce, I am glad that you never did and that is the secret success of our imperfect family. A legacy you have left not only for us but hopefully for your thirteen grandchildren. I hope we will continue to hold the permanency in marriage as our heritage.

Papa, you were committed to my having good handwriting despite the challenges I had holding a pen properly. You compelled me to write the same sentence 'umpteen' times while you were out all day (ha ha...). When I failed in my academics, you reassured me that I am intelligent and that "failure is part of success". I still recall your common proverbs when advising me "far away hills look green"; "Walls have ears" that "Pretense governs the world". I remember being bullied by some of your pupils who felt you were too strict on them and thought they could retaliate and take it out on me. You bought me novels to read that helped me to realize that I am unique and perfect the way God made me. Your words instilled and boosted my self-esteem until I realized my full picture through the mirror of God's word. You emphasized the importance of education, woke me up early in the morning to study and watched until I switched off my burning lantern to sleep. In the best way, you knew you drilled it into me that the only way out of poverty is getting a good education.

I watched you multitask as a teacher, headmaster, family nurse and 'village doctor.' I recall you waking me up at 5 am to assist in sterilizing the syringes and needles you need to treat your patients before they were seated in our house at 6 am. By 7 am or so you would jump on your bicycle to school expecting me to tidy up your injection care kit. You got to school before me and led the late coming team that spanked me for being late to school. Remember when you realized mathematics was not my thing? You asked my classroom teacher permission to teach his math class to ensure that I was able to understand arithmetic.

You inspired me to choose the nursing profession as my career in 1984 after my high school graduation—a time when nursing was not considered a noble profession as it is today. Papa, I saw how you cared for and honored Nene (Maternal Grandmother), the only Grandparent I knew. I appreciate your sacrificial involvement in offering a room in our house for her to live until her last few months of life. I will never forget when we celebrated her while she was alive and the befitting burial you gave her. The first time I saw apparent tears in your eyes was when the news of her death came to us. You instilled in me the essence of cleanliness, organization, and environmental safety as I remember you always picked up trash and warned against littering. You made your last round for the night ensuring that doors are locked, and our house is secured giving me a sense of protection that a good Father brings.

Mama, when I was in 3rd grade (elementary three) you made a courageous decision to stop your education after concerted effort to pursue higher education. I saw your enthusiasm and determination while you attended Obohia Technical Secondary School aspiring to obtain a vocational high school certificate. That ambition was aborted. I remember eavesdropping through the conversation you had with a dear uncle—Reverend Father Pius Iwuchukwu that culminated into you withdrawing from the school and waving higher education final goodbye to becoming a palm oil trader.

Perhaps there was more to the decision that I knew, but I do know this: as a result, you were there to love, teach and train me...to care for me and wipe my tears; to help me shop for textbooks, came to visit me in school. I will never forget my joy when you traveled all day by road to attend my matriculation/convocation at the then University of Ife, Nigeria without prior information of my room number or dorm address.

Mama, I can still picture the tears that rolled down your eyes at the bus stops at the beginning of each semester whenever we had to part for me to return to school. I remember how you used to sew for me; I think I was in early years of elementary school, when I cried my eyes out one Christmas Eve because there was no sign of a new dress for Christmas. Then came a "surprise" for me, a newly designed dress from your new fabrics. It turned out that you spent the night while I was asleep sowing for me. How could I forget my birthday celebrations with delicacies of my favorite dish, beans and rice with your designer stew? I will never forget the constant encouragement during teenage years; for teaching me about resiliency hard work and resolve. Though I never heard '*I love you*', I saw it sacrificially displayed.

Mama, you made sure that I attended all those catechism classes for baptism and confirmation, and that I always recited the prayers and hymns with you. You panicked when it seemed your daughter had become a 'religious fanatic'. Today we have come to find a common love in the Bible and that makes me the happiest woman on planet earth.

I listened to folktales, stories and watched all the drama skits that were a part of your elementary and middle school experiences. I always said with a sense of honor and pride how you completed 8-year elementary school (in those days) in 6 years because you were smart and teachers nominated you for double promotion.

I would always recall your account of disappointments including your dreams and wishes that never came to reality. Your love for higher education, which eluded you because of human selfishness and hatred. You would end your stories with praying that I never experienced such 'bad luck' and God listened to your heartfelt cries. My pursuit of a Ph.D. Degree despite the unspeakable hurdles I had to cross is in fulfillment of your longing for education. I did not want to settle for any terminal degree short of that and even with your failing strength and health you supported all the way, you never complained that I neglected you at times because of the high demand of completing my Ph.D. online and travels.

God works in mysterious ways. My faith, character, tenacity, hard work and resilience today is because of what I begrudgingly learned about the basics of the Christian faith in classes at St. Gregory parish and at home supporting you in farm work, palm fruit, palm kernel and cassava processing while attending most of my high school days from home. Though you had to take the double role of keeping multiple 'Susa' contributions running and maintaining our farm and fruiting plants, you were always available for me. You took the time to say nothing will stop me from getting a university degree even when you could no longer afford medicine for your high blood pressure and trendy clothes for public functions—you denied yourself membership to social clubs and events that would compel you to spend unnecessary money so that you could save up for our back to school necessities. Mama, you borrowed and borrowed, was insulted, threatened and stigmatized as stubborn because you did not want to be beaten twice. But hope wins!

To my four intelligent, industrious never giving up brothers we—have come a long way. You have kept our kinship in many respects and made my shortcomings easy to forget. Ours was the family that never had it all together but one just perfect enough for us. Despite the difficulties, all things good and bad have turned out for our good (Rom 8:28).

To our Trio—Onyedikachi, Chinonso and Amarachi. You have enriched my life of faith in Christ. You three are all truly an amazing bundle of inspiration. You keep the resounding melodious beats that resonate real hope in our home. I thank God for blessing my husband and I with you all!

To my husband of twenty-five years-NWANNEM. Thank you for taking me along this life journey. After my conversion and decision to commit to Christ, I had some reservations and unanswered questions. I thought practical Christianity was a fable until I met you. I am more appreciative than ever for your sacrificial involvement in my life. Our early years of marriage was without its crucible as I guess is expected from a marriage between two born-again believers in Christ and between two first-born children of Igboland. I may never know all your dedication and sacrifice, but I do know some; your presence at my mother's sickbed in Nigeria at a period you did not have to be there. Your faith in Christ that made you agree with me to fly my mother with apparent symptoms of a heart attack to the U.S. hoping for a miraculous healing and rescue. Your genuine and sincere faith in Christ that has made our house a home and an abode where laughing and singing have become our interior decoration.

The times you woke us up and taught us God's word and made the Bible relevant to every season of our marriage and parenting life. Your humility and selflessness that has made me continue to follow you as you followed Christ from college to the beautiful Columbia, Maryland. I also remember and thank you for the genuine support I received after encountering personal challenges while meeting nuclear and extended family needs. The hours you spent talking with me, exploring and surfacing my thoughts, feelings, ambitions and encouraging me until I took the last step in realizing my childhood dream of earning a Ph.D. degree. I thank you for believing and trusting me to travel far and near for both work and leisure.

On July 16, 1994, after I said, 'I do' I desired and hoped to be called Nwunye Prof' (Prof's wife) at some point in our marriage. A few years ago, that hope became a reality. I am married not only to Prof (as your Dad fondly called you) but also to the world-renowned Molecular Biologist and Plant Geneticist.

The best of all is that I am married to a Christian, a brother (Nwannem) and a true friend. I saw you grieve the passing of a sibling as well as my parents-in-law, Chief and Lolo Jacob and Beatrice Ude. You did not mourn as someone without hope. You are one of my constant reminders that hope in Christ is a win-win.

To you the reader, I hope the scriptural recipes, songs, personal stories and lessons that I shared in this book have driven your curiosities to considering Christ as a sure way out of despair. I hope you have an answer from this book to embrace the future with the attendant challenges. I pray you will resolve today to garnish your hope with an absolute surrender to Christ Jesus while you keep running, persevering, trusting and believing. *""Therefore, since we have a great high priest who has ascended into heaven, Jesus the Son of God, let us hold firmly to the faith we profess."* (Hebrews 4:14-16). Never give up on hope!

ABOUT THE BOOK

"Depressed and Despaired: The Synergy of Hope?" tells a true experience of hostilities and emotional trauma from relayed stories of underground bunker life including narrow escapes from frequent warplane bombs. From witnessed bitter aggressions, fracas and clashes from family and community relatives, academic failures, disappointments, sudden deaths of loved ones to embracing true Hope that changed the trajectory of a college student's life. In this personal story, there are many inspiring lessons and resourceful hope building tools acquired after a turning point with Christ. The narratives will inspire youths, students or anybody feeling depressed, discouraged, disappointed or contemplating to give up on life and to anyone who seeks bible-based resource for counseling and mentoring.

REFERENCE

Scriptural quotations are from the Holy Bible, New International Version. Grand Rapids: Zondervan House, 1984. Print.

OTHER RESOURCES

Age with Grace Health Services
 A faith-based health and wellness-focused seniors/older people's Day, Evening, Overnight Care, Assisted Living and Consultation Center.
Mission–Helping older loved ones celebrate a purposeful life as they age
Vision–Support older adults in aging through the promotion of balanced physical, social, mental and spiritual health.
Inquiries–Contact: isabbcommhealth@gmail.com

Flaws and Virtues: Tales for Moral Success
Life is a maze we all need to figure out. There could be flaws and virtues throughout this maze, but there is a MORAL way to success and you can learn from the stories of others! In this book, written by Amarachi, Chinonso and Onyedikachi Ude in a language that today's youths can relate to and understand.
Available on Amazon

www.ingramcontent.com/pod-product-compliance
Lightning Source LLC
Chambersburg PA
CBHW022129280326
41933CB00007B/608